Front Cover and Back Cover Description

Front Cover

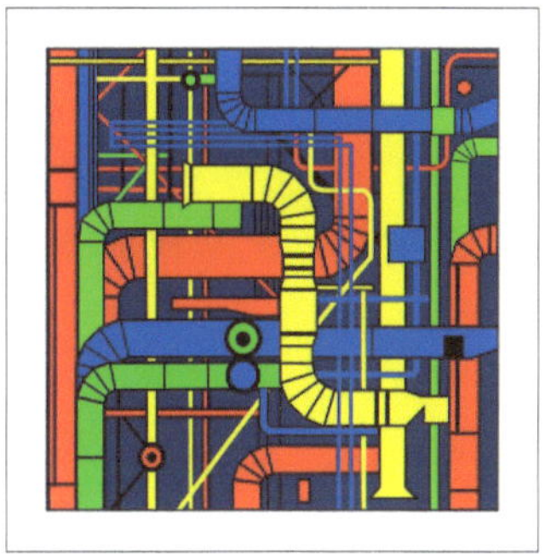

Le Centre George Pompidou Paris France

Asbjorn Lonvig's words: The most astonishing about The Centre National d'Art et de Culture Georges Pompidou is the backside architecture. Tubes painted in bright colors.
Wikipedia's words: The Centre national d'art et de culture Georges Pompidou was the brainchild of President Georges Pompidou who wanted to create an original cultural institution in the heart of Paris completely focused on modern and contemporary creation, where the visual arts would rub shoulders with theatre, music, cinema, literature and the spoken word. Housed in the centre of Paris in a building designed by Renzo Piano and Richard Rogers, whose architecture symbolizes the spirit of the 20th century, the Centre Pompidou first opened its doors to the public in 1977.
After renovation work from 1997 to December 1999, it opened to the public again on 1 January 2000, with expanded museum space and enhanced reception areas.
Since then it has once again become one of the most visited attractions in France.
Some 6 million people pass through the Centre Pompidou's doors each year, a total of over 190 million visitors in its 30 years of existence.

Back Cover

Photo and a few words about me
Pre-Introduction
ISBN
Bar Code

Contact Information:

Asbjorn Lonvig Art Books
Lille Fejringhus
43 Fejringhusvej
8722 Hedensted
DK-Danmark
lonvig@mail.dk
(+45) 75890477

Publishing Information:

Published by Asbjorn Lonvig Art Books
Printed by LuluPress
Raleigh North Carolina USA

ISBN 978-87-92419-32-3

Quick Response code (QR code)
lonvig.dk

Contents

Front Cover and Back Cover Description ——▶ 1
Front Cover information
Back Cover information
Contact and Publishing Information

By way of introduction
Pre-Introduction ——▶ 3
probably busy.
Drop "10 Dogmas" - just see the titles.
I recommend you read Introduction and Collection, too.

Introduction ——▶ 3 -4
I am a Software Engineer by IBM.
I was granted The World of Art Award.
Building on Gutenberg.
Chosen to represent Denmark at
2010 FIFA World Cup South Africa - started this concept.
Never before I have been able to print with
100% color matching combined with
400 years of sustainability.

The 10 IT-Dogmas ——▶ 5 - 12
Detailed technical description of the 10 IT-Dogmas to reach
the ultimate goal The World' Best in Fine Art...Nothing Less.
If you are busy just read the title of the 10 Dogmas.

Sample artworks and all 325+ motifs ——▶ 13 - 65
Samples enlarged and with a description.
All the 325+ motifs are shown as an overview
with thumbnails only.

Collecting ——▶ 66
Collecting and conclusion - I am a Lucky Bastard.
My new "Steinway & Sons" gives me the opportunity
to make the best artworks possible.

Next Step ——▶ 67
The natural continuation of this book is my website lonvig.dk ....
On lonvig.dk you will find thumbnails of all 325+ motifs -
click on a thumbnail and see enlargement and description of
a motif.

My Next Book "Art Beyond Bounds"——▶ 68

By Way of Introduction

Pre-Introduction

This book has two parts.

The first part is a *detailed* description of my 10 IT-Dogmas to reach the ultimate goal "The World's Best in Fine Art...Nothing Less".
The second part is about the 325+ artworks made according to the 10 dogmas, starting with 10 samples enlarged and described. Then all of the 325+ artworks are shown in small pictures - we call it thumbnails.

You are probably busy.
Then skip the detailed description of the 10 IT-Dogmas - it is rather technical.
Just read the titles of the 10 IT-Dogmas.
Then flick through the samples and thumbnails.
However.
I recommend that you read Introduction (p. 3-4) and Collecting (p. 66), too.

Introduction

Ten years ago or so, a French art magazine - the world leader in art market information - predicted that the art market would become 3.5 times larger than the present market due to the Internet. At that time, I had worked with art in traditional ways for several years. As well as being an artist, designer, etc.
I am a Software Engineer by IBM.
On the spot, I dropped traditional ways and started using computer and Internet in as many contexts as possible. All of my existing works were converted to digital format and all new works were created digitally.
Now, I would only use online galleries for exhibitions. I would only use traditional physical exhibition in my studio and gallery, and occasionally when online partner galleries organize physical exhibitions.

During the first years of using IT people from all over the world mocked me. I was surprised by the hateful rhetoric. I tried to enter into a dialogue, but nothing was to be discussed.

Time passed by, and digital art started to become nearly permissible. I was granted the World Art Award for my work in London, UK. I was granted two more awards, one in Rome and one in Montreal. I was appointed member of International Society of Artists and Designers in Rome. Critics compared me to Mondrian, Miró, Kandinsky, and Warhol. The French author Alain Johannes from Paris even compared me to the composer Johann Sebastian Bach. He wrote, "it takes a singular intent in the layout, in script, rudimentary forms of brightly colored."

Looking at Johann Sebastian Bach's work, I found out that he enriched the prevailing German music style with a robust contrapuntal technique, an unrivalled control of harmonic and motivic organization, and the adaptation of rhythms, forms, and textures from abroad, particularly from Italy and France. I believe that Alain Johannes's comparisons are about contrapuntal technique.

I had now passed the tipping point,
Digital art was not dubious anymore;
It was now kind of trendy.

Building on Gutenberg
However, I had one last huge problem; a problem that I believe was caused by Johann Gutenberg (1400-1468) from Mainz in Rheinland-Pfalz, Germany. His invention of mechanical movable type printing started the Printing Revolution and is widely regarded as the most important event of the modern period. This innovation played a key role in the development of the Renaissance, Reformation, and the Scientific Revolution. It also laid the material basis for the modern knowledge-based economy and the spread of learning to the masses.

But since Gutenberg's printing focused on printing text, the keywords minimized printing costs, optimizing speed, minimizing inking - and the overall focus was on minimizing costs. To the artist, the printing process has to do with pigmented inks, color calibration, fade, sustainability, and water resistance. Overall the result must be a high quality print and most important, sustainable.

South Africa
After I participated in "2010 International Fine Art" in South Africa, where digital artworks were printed on Hahnemühle paper using pigment-based archival inks a new world opened up to me as an artist. It was the first time I saw the phrase "pigment-based archival inks" in a digital environment. Now we may be solving "One last huge problem."
I had an idea to publish my best 325+ artworks and formulate 10 IT-Dogmas to reach the ultimate goal "The World's Best in Fine Art…Nothing Less."

Color Systems
This, of course, is subjective - not least because "The World's Best" is a subjective judgment. What is important to notice is, for the first time - and I mean the first time - I was able to print the exact colors that I wanted. Without exception, any kind of printing in the past has involved some kind of conversion of the colors to another color-system. The colors I normally use on my screen are in RGB. In order to print I had to convert to CMYK, or some other color-system. Even if you make lithography, you have to mix colors. Manufactured colors have never revealed the true beauty of the artwork.
Now I can calibrate my monitor and my printer using the Advanced Profiling System with validation.

Grandma Duck's Car

The grandma in Walth Disney's Donald Duck universe has a car like this - in Lille Fejringhus all of us are Donald Duck fans. We have a huge collection of Donald Duck booklets and all JUMBO books. We have seen all the Donald Duck cartoons. Among my children's toy cars I found the 1919 Ford High Body Model-T Coupe as a small model. The Ford Model T vehicle changed the thought and transportation patterns of Americans as surely as railroads had altered personal travel in the 1830s was the Ford Model T inexpensive and trustworthy, coupes like this 1919 model allowed people to go wherever they pleased.

The 10 IT-Dogmas
to reach the ultimate goal
The World's Best in Fine Art...Nothing Less.

The 10 IT-Dogmas – Titles Only

1. A High Quality Artwork created on computer/workstation/monitor in vector based graphic software, created traditionally and digitalized by photo or scanning, or by using software that generates the original automatically.

2. *A High Quality Projector connected online to the computer/workstation for dynamic decision on artwork sizes and general appearance.*

3. *A High Quality Medium that is high quality paper or high quality canvas.*

4. *Access to printer manufacturer's image performance laboratories as well as access to Wilhelm Imaging Research, Inc. for tests of quality and sustainability.*

5. *A High Quality Certificate of Authenticity.*

6. *A High Quality Hologram System.*

7. *High Quality Inks, which must be pigment-based archival inks.*

8. *A High Quality Printer from a major printer manufacturer.*

9. *High Quality software for managing calibration advanced profiling etc.*

10. *High Quality Aftercare using the most innovative choice in protective materials.*

Al Capone's Cadillac 1930 Chicago Illinois US

Alphonse Gabriel "Al" Capone (January 17, 1899 – January 25, 1947) was an American gangster who led a Prohibition-era crime syndicate The Chicago Outfit, which subsequently became known as the "Capones", was dedicated to smuggling and bootlegging liquor and other illegal activities such as prostitution, in Chicago from the early 1920s to 1931.
The Cadillac V-16 (sometimes known as the Cadillac Sixteen) was Cadillac's top-of-the-line car from its January 1930 launch until production ceased in 1940 as the war in Europe killed sales.
All were finished to custom order, and the car was built in very small numbers; only 4076 cars were constructed during the eleven years the model was offered. The majority of these were built in the single year of 1930, before the Great Depression really took hold. This was the first V16 powered car to reach production status in the United States.

The 10 IT-Dogmas - Details

1.

A High Quality Artwork created on computer/workstation/monitor in vector based graphic software, created traditionally and digitalized by photo or scanning, or by using software that generates the original automatically*.

The concept of Quality is very difficult to define when it comes to art.
We have no objective way to settle if an artwork is High Quality.
I choose to say that the judgment concerning my own works is mine.
I am very well aware that this judgment is subjective.
My subjective judgment is based on the response from others.
See "The Complete Fine Artworks of World of Art Award Winning Artist Asbjorn Lonvig, Denmark," which exhibits and describes every single artwork and "respond from others" (Critics and Testimonials).
The artwork is created by means of IT.
A computer with vector based graphic software like OpenOffice.org Draw, Paint Shop Pro 9, Paint Shop Pro Photo X3, Adobe Illustrator, MS Paint, MS Draw or others is used.
Vector based so that every single details of a motif can be re-sized.
For conversion to traditional painting style with visual strokes etc. and producing digital paintings the software Corel Painter Essential 4 and Corel Painting 11 is installed.
The workstation is a workstation with a 21.5-inch Wide screen LCD Monitor.
Graphic computing and resizing high amounts of pixels demands a workstation with considerable CPU power (Intel® Core™ i5-660 processor (3,33 GHz, 4 MB cache, 1333 MHz memory or similar) and a large RAM (4 MB). The hard disk must be large in order to store pictures (0.3 TB – 1 TB is equal to 1000MB).
For taking digital photos and for taking Full HD video for a new website and for a comprehensive You Tube presence a 18 Mb has been included in the concept.

*) *...software that generates the original automatically.*
This phenomenon is the subject of my next book, which is published on the publishing house Asbjorn Lonvig Art Books. I intend to write a book each time I encounter significant innovation in the IT and Art fusion.
I am researching *...software that generates the original automatically.* It seams at first glance extremely controversial. It is not. Everybody has an obligation, including artists, to keep track of new possibilities.
Like *the software that generates the original automatically* Michelangelo and Rembrandt often did not paint themselves.
Michelangelo: (Wikipeadia) Some authorities believe that it may have been executed by one of Michelangelo's pupils from a drawing by the master or was a direct imitation of his work.
Rembrandt (Wikipeadia) ...like many masters before him, he encouraged his students to copy his paintings, sometimes finishing or retouching them to be sold as originals, and sometimes selling them as authorized copies.
My pupil or student is my 10 Dogmas including the prerequisite IT-technique.
A great problem to some and a great joy for others.
It is a commonly known fact that IT solutions out competes traditional solutions.
If you are lover of traditional Art, and a lover of traditional methods, feel free to love and encourage this.
I surely will contain it. It is part of my history, my contemporary inspiration.
But to traditional art lovers I would ask amicably that you likewise will contain *...software that generates the original automatically.*

2.

A High Quality Projector for dynamic determination of artwork sizes and general appearance.

The Major Manufacturer Projector is connected to the workstation through a VGA cable. The projector image is displayed on a white traditional canvas 200 x 150 cm (78.7" x 59.1") or 300 x 225 cm (118.1" x 88.6"), depending on which size-spectrum you want to work in.
The canvas is placed on a traditional Mabef M/06 Studio Easel.
At any time in the creative process, you can determine the image size and value it on a screen of canvas in an environment simulating traditional method.

3.

A High Quality Medium, that is paper of high quality or canvas of high quality.

I use the same paper and canvas, as "2010 International Fine Art" project, which took place in June 2010 in South Africa. I have chosen Hahnemühle in southern Lower Saxony in Germany. Their range of products for Fine Art Printing is an award winning collection of genuine artist papers in a variety of surfaces, base weights and structures, including ink-jet printable canvases. Photographers and artists use Hahnemühle Fine Art products with a premium ink-jet coating for exclusive photography, digital artworks, and reproduction of art and photography in a superior gallery and museum standard. Hahnemühle's papers provide an impressive and unique way to combine the precision of digital print media with the wonderful grace of genuine artist papers made in a traditional way. All Hahnemühle's products meet the highest standards of color range, depth, contrast, rendering, and color gradation. This enables extraordinary print results. The close cooperation maintained with leading ink-jet printer manufacturers assures the universal compatibility of Hahnemühle's products.
Hahnemühle was founded in 1584 and they are the oldest German paper-makers manufacturing papers for traditional and digital artists. Since the founding of the company more than 400 years ago, a forward-looking attitude has formed the basis for continuous growth and the innovative strength of the company. Close cooperation with national and international partners enables speedy transformation of research results into new products. These are successfully marketed via a global distributor network.
My choice of paper and canvas is:
A. Hahnemühle Museum Etching 350 gsm is a natural white, 100% Cotton Rag, OBA free paper with a slight texture and a soft homogenous surface.
B. Hahnemühle Artist Canvas 340 gsm. Canvas Artist has an appreciable linen structure with a matte ink-jet coating. The ink-jet coating guarantees excellent image definition and color graduation.4. Access to printer manufacturer's image performance laboratories as well as access to Wilhelm Imaging Research, Inc. for tests of print quality and sustainability.

4.

Access to printer manufacturer's image performance laboratories as well as access to Wilhelm Imaging Research, Inc. for tests of print quality and sustainability.

Developing innovative, high-quality hardware, ink and paper that produce professional-quality, highly fade-resistant digital print is a priority for the printer manufacturer and is an important feature that differentiates the quality of The Major Manufacturer's digital printing systems from those of most of its competitors.

The Major Manufacturer's Image Permanence Labs. The printer manufacturer has two state-of-the-art image permanence labs in San Diego, California and Corvallis, Oregon with custom image permanence testing equipment. These labs develop new test procedures to better predict image permanence across a wide range of degradation mechanisms including light fade, ozone fade, humidity-fastness, and dark storage (thermal) fade.

The Major Manufacturer 's image permanence testing equipment covers a wide range of acceleration factors, and is temperature- and humidity-controlled in order to replicate and predict image permanence under conditions that are representative of how customers actually store and display prints. For fluorescent light fade, the permanence predictions in The Major Manufacturer's labs correlate very well to published Wilhelm Imaging Research, Inc.'s permanence test results.

The Major Manufacturer's image permanence testing equipment is highly specialized and cannot be readily duplicated without substantial investment. For example, typical light fade tests are performed at 23ºC and 50% relative humidity even in the presence of extremely bright illumination (up to 350 times brighter than typical room), which is difficult for equipment to achieve and maintain. Significant human training and resources are needed to appropriately generate samples, take periodic measurements, and check and calibrate the equipment operating conditions. Acceleration factors between 2.5X to 350X the normal assumed daily light levels are used to span the range between "real world but very slow" and "highly accelerated" test conditions. Depending on the test model, both fluorescent and xenon arc light sources are also used to simulate residential indoor and commercial application daylight window fade conditions.

Although there is no official industry standard yet for light fade testing, the printer manufacturer follows the general testing method developed and used by Wilhelm Imaging Research, Inc. (WIR), Grinnell, Iowa a leading image permanence test lab.

As a best practice, The Major Manufacturer regularly submits its inks and printers to the WIR labs for light fade and dark storage stability testing. When available, The Major Manufacturer uses WIR results as its primary substantiation for fade resistance claims on prints produced with The Major Manufacturer photo systems. See Wilhelm Imaging Research Inc. test methods and test results at wilhelm-research.com.

5.

A High Quality Certificate of Authenticity.

The Hahnemühle Certificate of Authenticity was designed to protect the security and genuineness of your limited edition artworks and reproductions on Hahnemühle paper and to reduce the risk of forgery. Each certificate is made of premium deckle edged mould made paper with a Hahnemühle watermark and fluorescent security fibers.

6.

A High Quality Hologram System.

Each certificate is – as mentioned above - made of premium deckle edged molder made paper with a Hahnemühle watermark and fluorescent security fibers. A serialized numbered hologram is added to the certificate. A second, identically numbered hologram is then applied to the reverse side of the artwork. The combination of certificate and hologram assures that each Certificate of Authenticity relates to one particular piece of art. Text and layout of the certificate can be created individually.

7.

High Quality Inks, which must be pigment, based archival inks.

The Major Manufacturer's 12-ink printing system, using Vivera pigment inks, features new 73 Chromatic Red ink. The Major Manufacturer's Designjet produces high-quality prints with smooth transitions and true neutral grays using the Quad-Black Ink set for a wide range of creative applications. In addition, the Gloss Enhancer achieves superior gloss uniformity and minimizes bronzing on most glossy photo papers. Ideal for photo and fine art print service providers, graphic designers, and commercial printers, the Designjet Photo Printer achieves print permanence of more than 200 years..

8.

A High Quality Printer from a major printer manufacturer.

Several Major Manufacturers have been considered. A few were excluded because of lack of sustainability. The Major Manufacturer has been chosen from an overall business point of view only – not a technically point of view. A major manufacturer was selected. As a Software Engineer by IBM I have made this kind of decisions before - very well knowing, that another manufacturer might have specific products that at the moment might be technically better. In a time span of 5 years, my decision always proved to be right. In this case, I just had to prove to myself that The Major Manufacturer meets all my demands. The printer in question is a wonder from the Major Manufacturer. There are not a lot of these printer wonders in the commercial market. When it comes to printing speed, use of ink etc. it's not a winner. You might say it is too expensive. When it comes to my demands as an artist, it is simply the best.

9.

High Quality software for managing calibration, advanced profiling etc.

The Designjet Photo Printer offers an enhanced Color Center tool that enables users to easily perform calibration and profiling tasks. Leveraging the built-in embedded spectrophotometer and DreamColor technologies, users can easily generate custom International Color Consortium (ICC) profiles in-house under specific environmental conditions and create paper presets for the Designjet printer. The DreamColor Technologies, together with the embedded spectrophotometer, greatly simplifies accurate color matching and profiling. Professionals ultimately save time and effort by easily and consistently producing the colors they envisage are important, that the printer supplier works together with paper-makers in order to achieve the best result possible. On Hahnemühle's website www.hahnemuehle.com the ICCs for the Designjet and both Museum Etching 350 gsm and Artist Canvas 340 gsm are ready for free download.

10.

A High Quality Aftercare using the most innovative choice in protective materials.

Protective Spray is my choice in protective materials. The Hahnemühle Protective Spray offers incredible protection for your valuable ink-based images. This odorless spray seals the printed surfaces and protects them from dirt, fingerprints, and moisture. It increases the water-resistance of printouts and protects images from fading caused by UV rays. The Protective Spray is fast drying and does not turn yellow. It is completely transparent and has no influence whatsoever on the original colors of the paper. Hahnemühle Protective Spray probably doubles colorfastness.

Chinese for Fish

Some Chinese letters are very inspiring. Often one letter is a word like Fish above. The letters, that describe a word then are interpreted by adding colorful simplicity.

The adding of the style colorful simplicity continues the story of the Chinese letter.

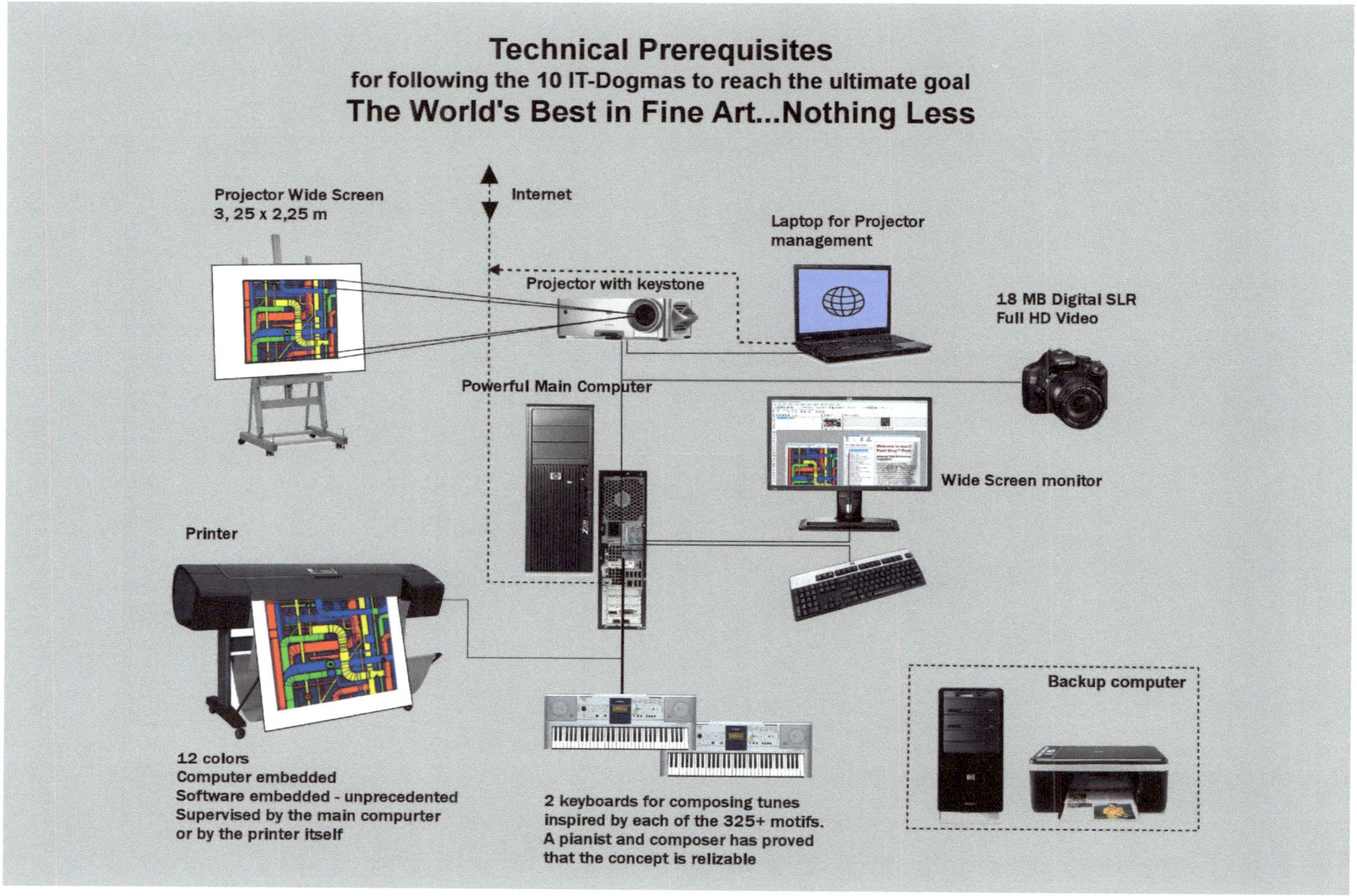
Technical Prerequisites
for following the 10 IT-Dogmas to reach the ultimate goal
The World's Best in Fine Art...Nothing Less
Projector Wide Screen
3, 25 x 2,25 m
Internet
Laptop for Projector
management
Projector with keystone
18 MB Digital SLR
Full HD Video
Powerful Main Computer
Wide Screen monitor
Printer
Backup computer
12 colors
Computer embedded
Software embedded - unprecedented
Supervised by the main compurter
or by the printer itself
2 keyboards for composing tunes
inspired by each of the 325+ motifs.
A pianist and composer has proved
that the concept is relizable

Technical Prerequisites

for following the 10 IT-Dogmas to reach the ultimate goal
The World's Best in Fine Art...Nothing Less

See the drawing

1. Mabef M/06 Studio Easel.
2. Wide Screen on Canvas – enlargeable to Canvas size 2,25 x 4 m (88.6" x 157.5").
3. Designjet Photo Printer with 12 Pigment Ink Cartridges mounted simultaneously, and with an automatic calibration system.
4. Projector with keystone facilities.
5. Workstation/Computer with large range of software.
6. Laptop Projector manager.
7. Wide Screen Monitor with an automatic calibration system.
8. 18 Mb digital SLR Camera with full HD video capabilities.
9. 2 x YAMAHA Digital Keyboard PSR-E323
10. Backup computer and printer.

Samples

A number of samples showing enlarged motifs along with a comprehensive description.

Followed by an overview over the 325+ motifs presented as thumbnails (small pictures).

Chapel of Saint Louis des Invalides

Napoleon Bonaparte's final resting place underneath the Chapel of Saint Louis des Invalides . He died in St. Helena, a small remote island where the British placed him, and was originally buried there. Later, his remains were brought back to France and placed in a large red porphyry sarcophagus. Six more caskets line the inside, which become smaller, and the last one contains the remains of the emperor. Inside the Dome Church, you'll also find the tombs of his brothers, son, and other important military persons.

Rapa-Nui Moai

Moai

Easter Island is a Polynesian island in the south eastern Pacific Ocean, at the most south eastern point of the Polynesian triangle. The island is a special territory of Chile. Easter Island is famous for its monumental statues, called moai, created by the Rapa-Nui people. It is a world heritage site with much of the island protected within the Rapa-Nui National Park.

Easter Island is known by the locals as Rapa-Nui and it has just one town, Hanga Roa where virtually every one of the 2,700 inhabitants lives.
The island is roughly triangular in shape with an extinct volcano at each corner.

This collection of 25 meter-high stone sculptures still puzzles historians and archaeologists as to their origin. It is believed that a society of Polynesian origin settled here in the 4th century and established a unique tradition of monumental sculpture. Between the 10th and 16th centuries, they erected the enormous stone figures, known as the Moai, which have long fascinated the entire world and endowed this island with a mythical atmosphere.

Easter Island was discovered on Easter Sunday, 1722 by the Dutch explorer Jakob Roggeveen.
The history of Easter Island is rich and controversial. Its inhabitants have endured famines, epidemics, civil war, slave raids and colonialism, and the crash of their ecosystem. The population has declined precipitously more than once. They have left a cultural legacy that has brought them fame disproportionate to their population.
Contemporary to the arrival of the first settlers of Hawaii, 300-400 CE was published as a date for initial settlement of Easter Island. Although some scholars argue for initial settlement of 700-800 CE, there is an on-going study by archaeologists Terry Hunt and Carl Lipo that states: “Radiocarbon dates for the earliest strati-graphic layers at Anakena, and analysis of previous radiocarbon dates imply that the island was colonized late, about 1200 CE. Significant ecological impacts and major cultural investments in monumental architecture and statuary thus began soon after the initial settlement.”

The Birdman legend

9 Oncor-Hynchus-My-Kiss

Oncor-Hynchus-My-Kiss

HI, my name is Oncor-Hynchus-My-Kiss.
That's Latin and it means Rainbow Trout.
Just call me My-Kiss.
I crossed the Atlantic Ocean from North America in 1885.
I was just an egg then.
I was hatched in Denmark and since then I was a Fish Farming Fish.

However, I have not been successful all the time.
In some periods my colors are transformed into grey nuances.
I am confused and I swim in the wrong direction.
I am depressed.
My name is Oncor-Hynchus-My-Kiss-Atrox-Grisea-Digitalis-Rubra,
which is the Latin for the Terrible Grey Rainbow Trout?
bringing about Red Figures in the accounts.
During these periods it is not fun at all to be a Rainbow Trout.
During these periods it is not fun at all to be a Fish Farmer or the processing industry.
In other periods, however, I'm successful...

...and in other periods my colors are transformed into golden nuances.
Auratus starts with the letters AU - the chemical symbol for gold.
Auratus is Latin for gold.
Fish Farmers and the processing industry consider me as a pure GOLDFISH.
Fish farmers and the people in the processing industry are sedate people
who do not use big words.
It is certainly from these periods the Danish phrase "not so bad after all" originates.
Dantrout was started by a group of visionary Fish Farmers*.
And Dantrout has always been very closely related to fish farming.
Dantrout has been in a bit of everything.
Ups and downs.
At some point Dantrout was actually owned by Royal Greenland...

I and Dantrout now live nicely and brightly.
Sometimes my colors turn into beautiful arctic blue colors and white.
White as the arctic ice.
I got the name Oncor-Hynchus-My-Kiss- Arcticus-Azure.
I was so happy because I believe Royal Greenland is the world's best brand.
However.
I was hit by disease. Very serious illness - I was near death.
The new owners bought Dantrout in order to give me a dignified death.
However, the new owner's further explorations revealed new potentials in Dantrout.
I and Dantrout survived.

This time, the nuances are in green.
I have got the lovely name Oncor-Hynchus-My-Kiss-Ecológica.
Dantrout is building an ultra visionary fish farm not far from the Brande area,
where Dantrout was founded.

Dantrout works together with the innovative owner of Kærhede Fish Farm in Kibæk.
This new fish farm needs no river – no creek.
A little crazy, don't you think?

A fish farm where the water is from the underground and pumped back into the underground through an ingenious system of pipes.
There is a filtering through naturally occurring coal seams.
A fish farm, which could be placed in your living room, no environmental impact at all.
A fish farm where the sludge is collected….
By burning the sludge pure phosphorus (P) is generated.
The letter P in NPK fertilizer.
A fish farm, where everything is controlled technologically.
A fish farm where the feeding is monitored on TV via cameras located in the basin bottom to ensure proper food intake to ensure our well-being.

A fish farm with 72 tanks inside a house, divided into separate units with 6 pools, where one unit can be shut down and cleaned separately.
As Oncor-Hynchus-My-Kiss-Ecológica I am helping to keep the planet clean.
I increase Dantrout's production by 50% and I help to ensure Dantrout's future commodity supply.
I am a proud Oncor-Hynchus-My-Kiss-Ecológica.
I am a proud Oncor-Hynchus-My-Kiss-Ecológica when the Minister for the Environment* in a few days passes by to visit me and to see our innovative organic project.

Sincerely,
Oncor-Hynchus-My-Kiss-Ecológica

*) I was born in Brande. My Grandfather Kristian Jensen was a prosperous Fish Farmer. Believe it or not - he was one of the visionary Fish Farmers, who started Dantrout in 1939 - then it was called Dansk Andels Ørredseksport.

*) The Minister of the Environment is called Troels.
As a politician he is considered dull and grey.
However.
He visits me now and then.
We attend soccer matches together - we are fans of the same soccer team.
In these cases he is bubbling and colorful.
When the opponent to our soccer team scores a goal he cries out loudly "Oh Shit", "Damn It"…….
He has promised to arrive in his distinguished ministerial car with a driver next time he visits me.

My own fairy tale characters

Fairy Tale Characters
They are the actors in my fairy tales. I have written and published several. Some of the fairy tales have been translated and published into 15 languages.
The fairy tale characters have been used for a lot of other things. Posters, postcards, T- shirts, bags, shoes, boots, clocks, curtains, beddings and sheets - you Name-It.
Even US Postal stamps.
The giraffe is called Tall-Charlie - he is the most popular.
25 Congratulations is a present for Bestseller's children's clothes brand Name-It on the occasion of Name-It's 25th birthday.
I presented the concept to Name-It. Name-It told me that if there had been no economical crisis, then we would have started a children's clothes collection based on my characters tomorrow.
I have promised Name-IT not to offer my fairy tale concept to another children's clothes producer.
Name-It is in my opinion the only company in Denmark that has the necessary financial strength to commercialize my fairy tale concept worldwide.

Blue Sky - Guggenheim New York

Blue Sky

New York is yellow cabs, black people, white people, red lights, green lights, noise, Hotel Lexington, homeless, alcohol, narcotics, penthouses, Fifth Avenue, Thumps Tower, Metropolitan, restaurants, delis, Central Park, backyards, glory, misery, China Town, Rockefeller Centre, millionaires, beggars, subways, Broadway, tourists, diplomats, UN......

But New York is not really New York without Guggenheim, the great Art Museum on Fifth Avenue. The architect is Frank Lloyd Wright.
It is one of Frank Lloyd Wright's two masterpieces.
The second masterpiece is Fallingwater, Bear Run, Pennsylvania, a house placed magnificently in a butiful landscape.
A creek is running through the house!
Amazing how Frank Lloyd Wright's architecture is contemporary.
In Chicago I saw several of his houses in Oak Park that looked as if they were built yesterday.
One was from 1909.

He himself lived in Oak Park, Studio at 951 Chicago Avenue.
I saw it.
It is designed by him.
Early in his career.

Frank Lloyd Wright had for sure a rare gift.

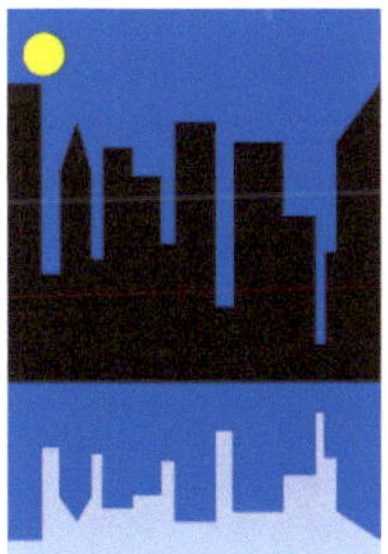

Manhattan New York

Soul Hurting Still

Soul Hurting Still

The jubilation feelings given by forms and colors of Asbjorn Lonvig

French author Alain Johannes from Paris praises Asbjorn Lonvig's art to the skies in his new book
"Comment communiquer par des images". It was presented at "Salon du Livre" in Paris.

He has written the following about me and "Soul Hurting Still":
The art of the Danish painter Asbjorn Lonvig communicates at the first glance euphoria in a rough state.
A so intense euphoria that the glance cannot move away from the piece of his art.
Of course, the saturated colors are decisive in this very great glowing.
The colored dazzling and the feeling of pleasure which prolongs it have multiple causes.
As adequacy between artistic creation and the constraints of communication, the art of Asbjorn Lonvig
Illustrates an assumption of neuron cognitive sciences: the neurons in charge of visual perception are first activated by patterns recognition, then by colors recognition, then by recognition of textures and movements recognition. In a piece of art like "Soul hurting still ", the sensory impacts of the forms and the colors are very strong and equal. The pleasure comes from what the eye and the brain receive from the red, the yellow, the green and blue at the same time as they recognize the squares, the rectangles, the circles, the triangles, the straight and broken lines and even the letter "A".
The glance thus filled by a profusion of feelings founds a generating mental state of pleasure.
After and beyond the primary emotion, in a second phase of contemplation, the spirit endeavors to confer an overall significance on the table. It calls upon its repertory of already memorized forms. Then, the pleasure becomes ludic. Functioning like a rebus, the chart of an unknown territory, a coded language or a mysterious diagram, the piece of art asks to the witness: "What am I?"
The many possible answers are mental resonances which give to the artistic communication richness higher than all the other ways to communicate.
This communication is inter subjective. It organizes the meeting between the subjectivity of the artist and the subjectivity of the witness.
The witness of the piece of art is free to refer to tropical sensory prints: association of a dominating solar yellow, sky blue, deep vegetal green. He can also associate the table with an intimate collection of primitive art.
He shall perhaps remember the geometrical abstractions of Kandinsky and Mondrian. Surely, the piece of art will be kept in the long memory space into the brain with all its resonances sensory, emotional, ludic and cultural.
It is may be interesting to know that the joyful impact piece of art by Asbjorn Lonvig is closely related to its canvassed artistic. High level data processing specialist then head of a software company, the painter found serenity in a pictorial creation which starts with digital drafts and finds its completion on a support – frame and fabric - entirely conceived and manufactured by the artist.

Alain Johannes, Author
Paris, France

Spanish Bull

Museo del Prado Madrid Spain

Spanish Bull.

Inspired by bullfighting.
Bullfighting is a traditional spectacle of Spain, Portugal, some cities in southern France, and several Latin American countries, in which one or more live bulls are ritually killed in a bullring as a public spectacle.

Bullfighting generates heated controversy in many areas of the world, including Mexico, Ecuador, Spain, and Portugal.
Supporters of bullfighting argue that it is a culturally important tradition, while animal rights groups argue that it is a blood sport because of the suffering of the bull and horses during the bullfight.

According to DACS in UK, which is a sister organization to Copy-Dan, who administers artists' intellectual rights in Denmark, the copyrights for this motif costs a fortune – or 2.
An English company wanted to buy the copyrights for a particular purpose – a particular product - and DACS priced the non-exclusive copyright £ 40,000!

Sagrada Familia Barcelona Spain

Sydney Opera House Sydney Australia

The Blue Kangaroo

Sydney Opera House

The architecture of this house is known worldwide, but did you know the architect is one of my Danish fellow citizens. Jorn Utzon is his name. However Utzon resigned from this job after 9 years of building. Since then, Utzon has never returned to Australia to see his famous building finished.
As Utzon was looking for an ideal refuge, he built the house "Can Lis" in 1972, with an extraordinary view to the sea. A house with huge windows without glass - inviting nature indoor.
Like Frank Lloyd Wright designed the Falling water in Bear Run, Pennsylvania - Utzon designed his gem "Can Lis" in Porto Pietro, on the Spanish island Mallorca.
We went into the opera house to see and hear a Spanish version of Carmen.
Carmen is a French “opéra comique” by Georges Bizet.
The opera premiered at the Opéra-Comique of Paris on 3rd March 1875, but its opening run was denounced by the majority of critics.
It was almost withdrawn.
Bizet died on 3rd June 1875, never knowing how popular Carmen would become.
The story is set in Seville, Spain, c. 1830, and concerns the eponymous Carmen, a beautiful Gypsy with a fiery temper. Free with her love, she woos the corporal Don José, an inexperienced soldier. Their relationship leads to his rejection of his former love, mutiny against his superior, and joining a gang of smugglers. His jealousy when she turns from him to the bullfighter Escamillo leads him to murder Carmen.
In the opera I sat together with my family behind a large lady who had emptied several bottles of perfume immediately before the performance. We endured the stench for a long, long first act.
A unanimous decision was made as soon as we reached the interval.
We left.
Our love to Utzon, to Carmen, to Bizet could not in any way overshadow the fat lady’s odors.
The keywords for my inspiration to “Sydney Opera House” thus was Utzon’s fantastic architecture in Sydney, Carmen and Georges Bizet, Spain and Spanish. (Notice: Colors of ***"Sydney Opera House"*** are equivalent to colors in ***“Spanish Bull”***).
I hope I managed to leave out the large lady.

The large Lady
Asbjorn Lonvig's words: Having read the lyrics, having heard and seen Joe Tex on YouTube, I imagine a very, very large lady dancing.
Sony's words: Artist: Joe Tex, Written by Buddy Killen and Bennie McGinty,

Think Wind Power

Think Wind power

I'm a member of "Organizing for America" supporting Barack Obama's ideas.
Every second day I receive news about his doings and whereabouts.
Barack Obama believes we have a moral, environmental, economic, and security imperative to address our dependence on foreign oil and tackle climate changes in a serious, sustainable manner.
I'm a Dane, you know.

I was raised in a country where we could see a windmill in whatever direction we looked.
Decades ago the windmills were used for milling grain.

Now they produce energy for multiple purposes.
The Danish wind turbine industry is the world's largest.
The global company Siemens' Headquarters for Wind Energy has thus been placed in Brande, Denmark.
I work together with Siemens Wind Power in Brande.

"Think Wind Power" is inspired by *Gyro Gearloose's** Little Helper, Barack Obama's ideas, Siemens Wind Power and myself, who are environmentalists by conviction.

*) Gyro Gearloose is an inventor appearing in comic book stories as a friend of Donald Duck.
Gyro is often assisted by his Little Helper (or just "Helper"), who is a small anthropomorphic robot with a light bulb as a head symbolizing genius.

Sunrise in Eastern Spain

Toulouse

Toulouse

Henri de Toulouse-Lautrec (1864 – 1901) was a French painter, printmaker, draftsman, and illustrator, whose immersion in the colorful and theatrical life of fin de siècle Paris yielded an oeuvre of exciting, elegant and provocative images of the modern and sometimes decadent life of those times. Toulouse-Lautrec is known along with Cézanne, Van Gogh, and Gauguin as one of the greatest painters of the Post-Impressionist period.

At the age of 13 Henri fractured his right thigh bone, and at 14, the left. The breaks did not heal properly. Modern physicians attribute this to an unknown genetic disorder.
His legs ceased to grow, so that as an adult he was only 1.22 m (4 ft 6 in) tall, having developed an adult-sized torso, while retaining his child-sized legs, which were 0.70 m (27.5 in) long.
Toulouse-Lautrec gave himself up fully to the bohemian life, spending much of his time drinking and carousing - and constantly sketching - in cabarets, racetracks, and brothels.

I was at an exhibition at an art museum. The exhibition was called “Hommage á Henri Toulouse-Lautrec”.
I have been always fascinated by Henri de Toulouse-Lautrec - for thousands of reasons.
One of them is Toulouse-Lautrec's first poster, *Moulin Rouge - La Goulue*, which introduced poster design a bold simplification of form, space, and composition learned from Japanese woodblock prints.

I met him in Moulin Rouge in Paris once. He sure was drunk. Was I?

“Hommage” means “in honor of” and I saw no honor at all.
I had nothing to do but go home and create my own *“Hommage á Henri Toulouse-Lautrec”.*

My inspiration: His art, his hat, his glasses, his beard, his small legs, his clothes. The red scarf is not his own. It is a part of my imaginable perception of Henri Toulouse-Lautrec.
Be sure, it is the scarf of Aristide Bruant on one of Henri Toulouse-Lautrec’s most famous posters.

Moulin Rouge Paris

Perception I

Perception II

TOPTEN

Exhibition in Rome, Italy at ARTROM Gallery Guild, November 30th 2011 to January 15th 2012.

The ARTROM Gallery GUILD in Rome is a world-wide showcase of outstanding artists and designers.

All AGG Members were selected as Winners of an ARTROM Gallery Competition, or they applied to become a member, and were accepted through a jury review.

ARTROM Gallery has decided to dedicate the first exhibition in the season to the presentation of artists who were chosen as winners or finalists in ARTROM Gallery's previous International Art Competitions.

ARTROM Gallery Guild: "We are impressed with your work. For this exhibition we would be interested in presenting your prints."

I am one of the 10 selected artists.

I'll show works with the theme "Perception".

Perception

Wikipeadia, the free encyclopedia:
Perception is the process of attaining awareness or understanding of the environment by organizing and interpreting sensory information. All perception involves signals in the nervous system, which in turn result from physical stimulation of the sense organs.

*English writer and dramatist Douglas Adams (*1952)*
Everything you see or hear or experience in any way at all is specific to you. You create a universe by perceiving it, so everything in the universe you perceive is specific to you.

*Swiss psychiatrist C. G. Jung (*1875):*
The essence of C. G. Jung's theory on perception is that much seemingly random variation in behavior is actually quite orderly and consistent, being due to basic differences in the way individuals prefer to use their perception and judgment.

*Chinese Philosopher Confucius (*551 BC):*
Everything has beauty, but not everyone sees it.
To know is to know that you know nothing. That is the meaning of true knowledge.
When we see men of a contrary character, we should turn inwards and examine ourselves.

Symbolism

I have made these works because I want to establish perception which psychologically and philosophically is one of the most important issues to humanity.

The artwork consists of 2 motifs.

2 motifs which seen separately are seemingly identical.

However, if you look closer you will realize that they are not – not at all.

Few elements are identical – the theme is the same but the actual shapes are not.

They symbolize different perceptions of the same incident or object.

They symbolize that two or more incidents or objects will be conceived differently by different human beings when their sense organs, like sight, hearing, sense of smell etc. are stimulated.

Everything an individual sees, hears, smells etc. or experiences in any way at all is specific to that individual.

Perception is the outcome of the individual's inherence and experiences to make things orderly and consistent.

People must accept the individuality of perception.

Perception is individual and questionable.

Perception is not to know.

Perception is to know nothing.

To know is to know that you know nothing

Colorful Circles

Colorful Circles

Think of a Paris Wheel.
Think of Jung and one of his mandalas.
Think of Niels Bohr and how electrons in an atom are whirling around the nucleus.
Think of a sandwich cake.
Think of what happens if the sun shines on to droplets of moisture in the atmosphere.
Think of cycling with a punctured tire
Think of the joyful Buddhist's Wheel of Life.
Think of the circle which inspired the development of geometry, astronomy, and calculus.
Think of that the wheel was connected to the divine in the Late Middle Ages.
Think of that the wheel was invented in the 4th millennium BC
Think of the joy mankind had has since 4th millennium BC if the wheel had not been invented.

These thoughts are collected in "Colorful Circles".

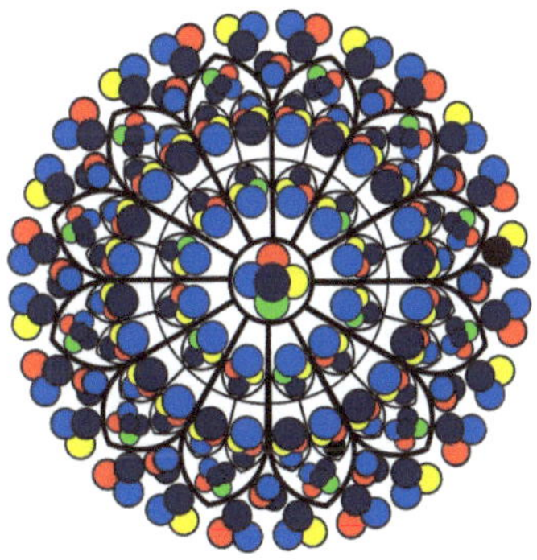

The South Rose
A small story about the South Rose. I am developing a seminar with the goal to improve creativity together with Stephen Burke, who is a psychologist with great experience in applied psychology and C. G. Jung. Unfortunately the seminar has been postponed. Stephen was headhunted by Lego. One day I showed my artwork "South Rose" to Stephen, and at the same time I asked him if it might be a mandala? He told me the South Rose stained glass window in Notre Dame de Paris was an illustration in one of C. G. Jung's books...sure, it is a mandala, Stephen said.

The 325+ motifs – 10 collections

I have selected the 325+ of my motifs and put them for sale produced according to the 10 IT-Dogmas. The 325+ motifs are categorized in collections:

The Abstract Collection
Abstract motifs in genre Colorful Simplicity

The North Europe Collection
Paris
Tour de France 2010
Tour de France 2011
London
Amsterdam - Berlin - St. Petersburg
Denmark - Hedensted - Brande - Vejle - The Little Belt Bridge - Funen

The South Europe Collection
Italy - Portofino - Sienna - Florence - Venice - Assisi - Paestum - Puglia
Rome - Coliseum - The Vatican - The Roman Forum - Pantheon - Museo Nazionale Romano
Spain - Madrid - Barcelona - Costa Brava - Granada - Lisbon – Porto

The North America Collection
Canada West - Canada East
New York – Buffalo
Chicago - Denver - Portland - San Francisco -
Grand Canyon - Nashville

The South America Collection
Caminito - Buenos Aires
Easter Island (Chile)

The East and far East Collection
Japan - Golden Pavilion - Tokyo Tower - Ginza - Fuji - Tokyo Portal
China - Confucius - Shanghai - Pudong - Wild Goose Pagoda - Temple of Longhua - Great Wall of China - Calligraphy
India - Taj Mahal
Nepal - Mount Everest

The Australia/Oceania Collection
Sydney Opera House – Kangaroo Canbara – Great Barrier Reef

The Africa Collection
South Africa - FIFA

The Miscellaneous Collection
Architecture
Circus
Museums - Cathedrals - Churches – Christianity
Hans Christian Andersen illustrations
Sculptural/Aesthetic: Vintage Cars - Racing Cars - Motor Cycles
Wind Power
Flowers
Fairy Tale Characters from my Fairy Tales
Special Selection: Visual Knowledge - Lonvig by Minymo - Dantrout

The Owner's Collection
Only for sale to the owners.

The Abstract Collection

Colorful Simplicity

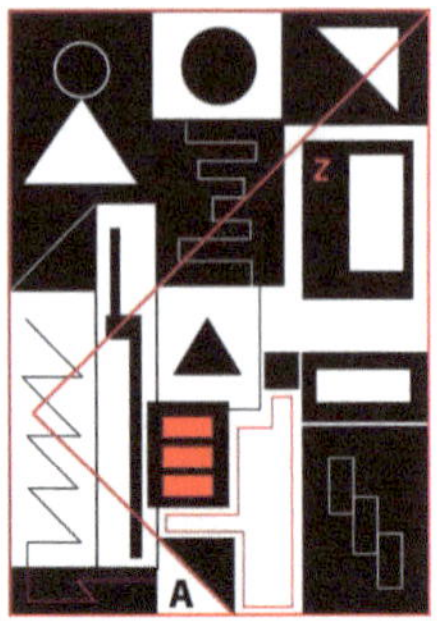
Z
A
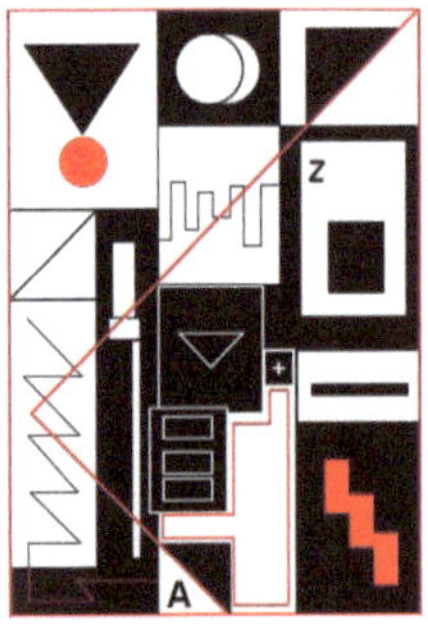
Z
A
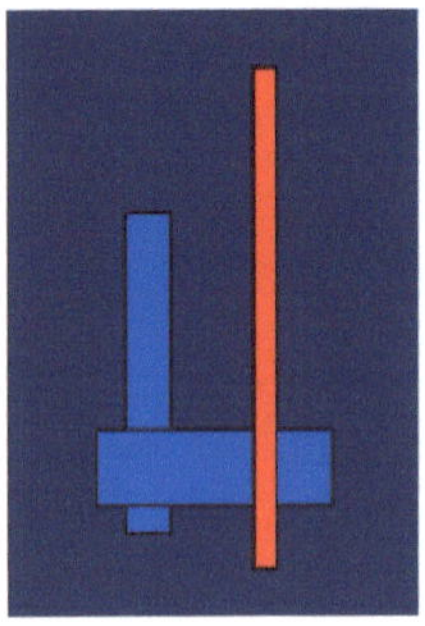

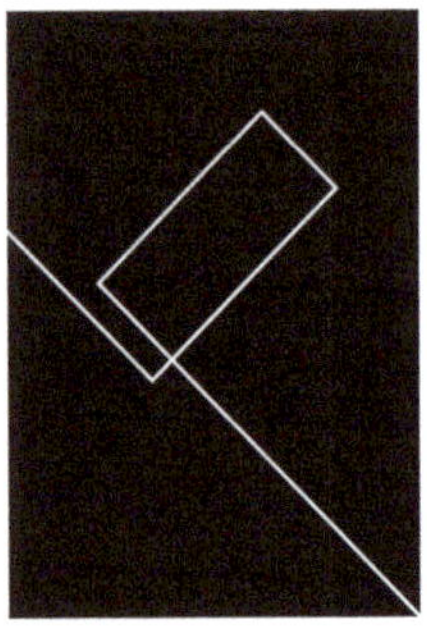
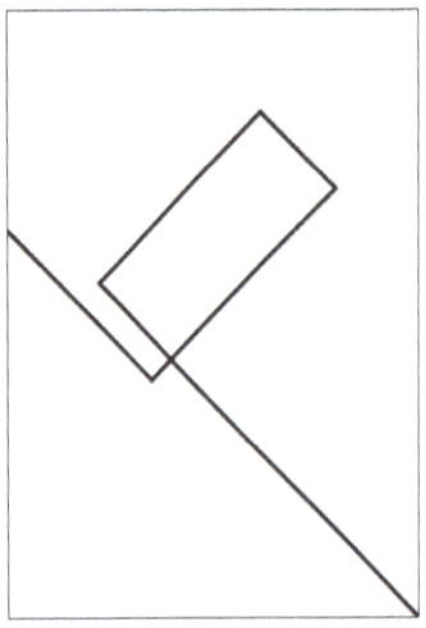

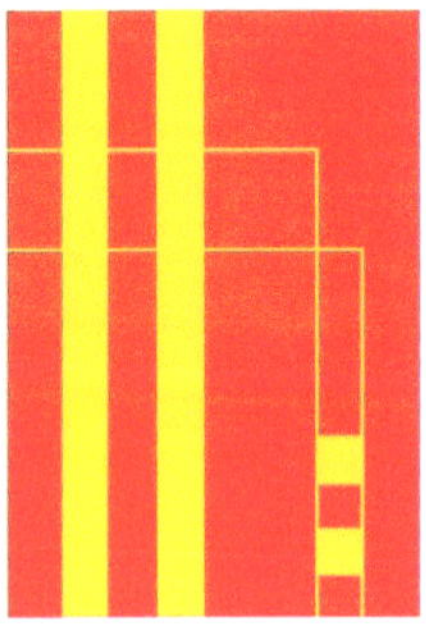
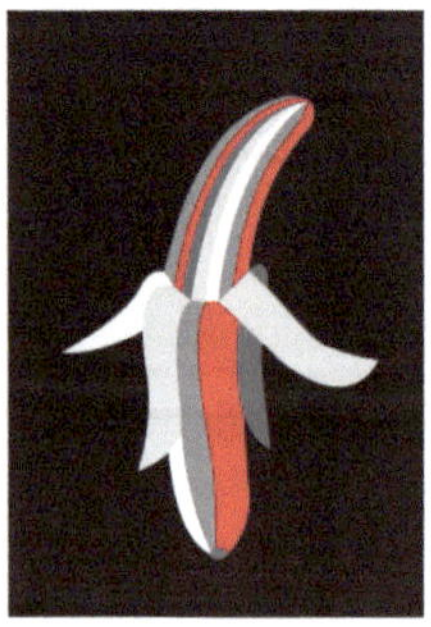

The North Europe Collection

Paris - Tour de France - Giro d'Italia - La Vuelta
London
Amsterdam - Berlin - St. Petersburg
Denmark - Hedensted - Brande - Vejle - The Little Belt – Funen

Paris

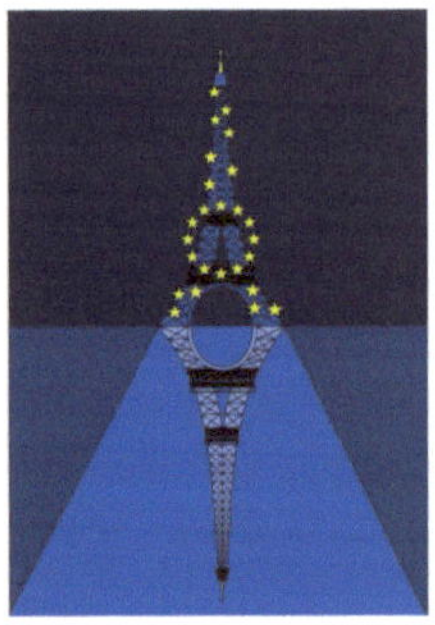

6
MAILLE
6
Moutardes & Condiments
Vinaigres & Cornichons

Tour de France - Giro d'Italia - La Vuelta

London

Amsterdam - Berlin - St. Petersburg

Denmark - Europe/North Africa, Denmark

Hedensted - Svends Mølle - Brande - Vejle - Vejle - Give - The Little Belt – Funen

The South Europe Collection

Italy - Portofino - Sienna - Florence - Venice –
Assisi - Paestum – Puglia

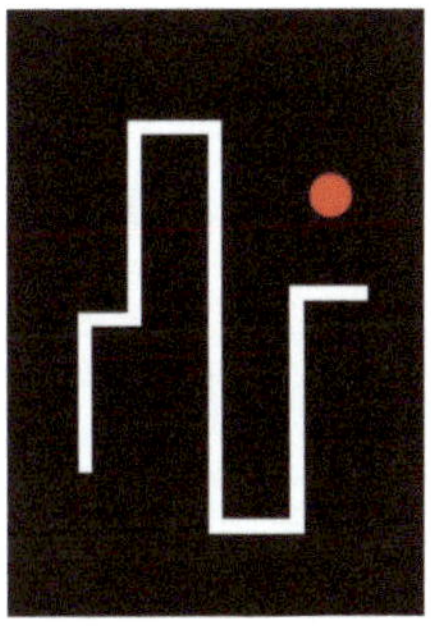

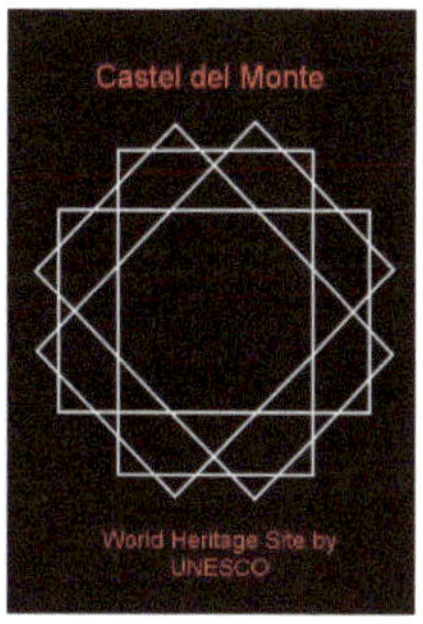

Rome - Coliseum - The Vatican - The Roman Forum

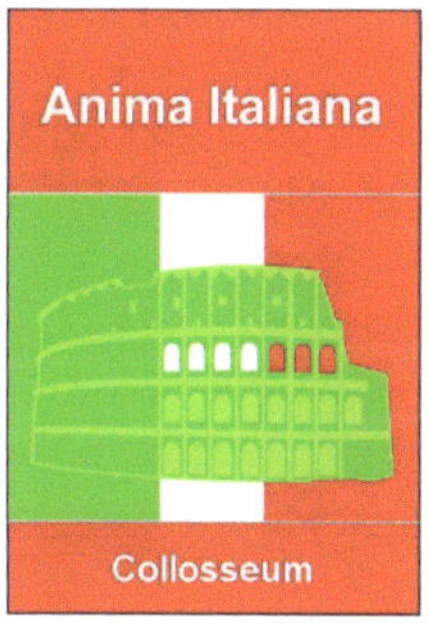

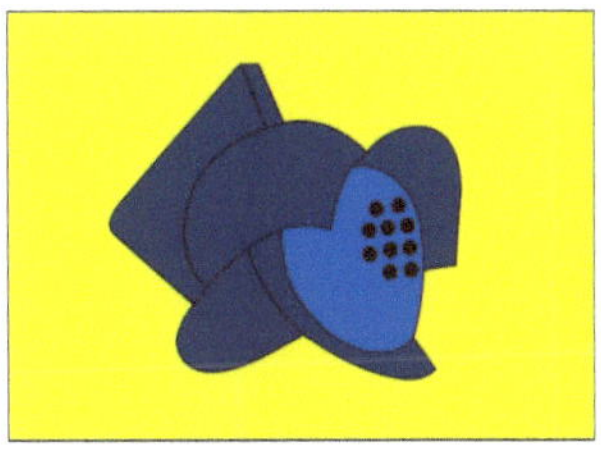

Rome - Pantheon - Muse Nazionale Romano Palazzo Massimo

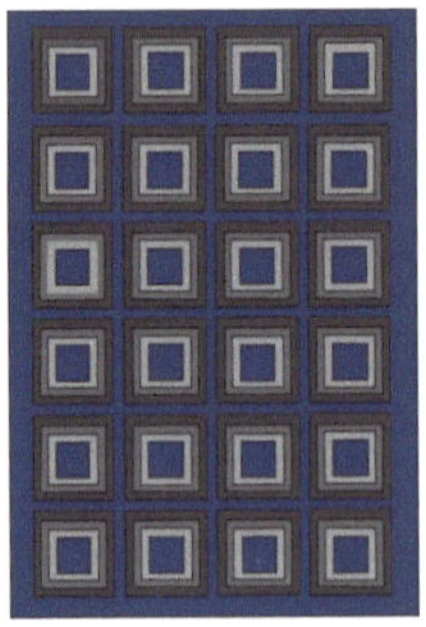

Spain - Madrid - Barcelona - Costa Brava - Granada - Lisbon – Porto

Spain

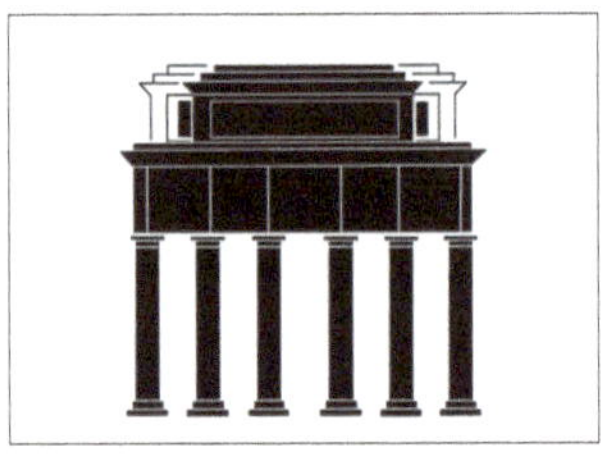

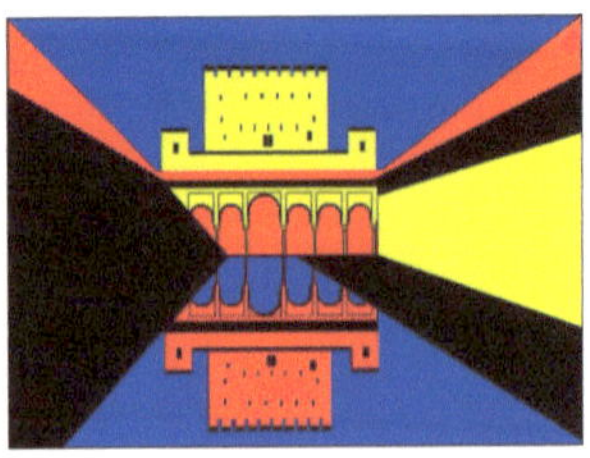

Portugal
Lisbon - Porto

The North America Collection

Canada West
Banff - Vancouver - British Columbia - Queen Charlotte Sound - Point Queen Charlotte

Canada East
St. Catharines near Niagara Falls - Toronto - St. Margarets Bay Nova Scotia - Halifax

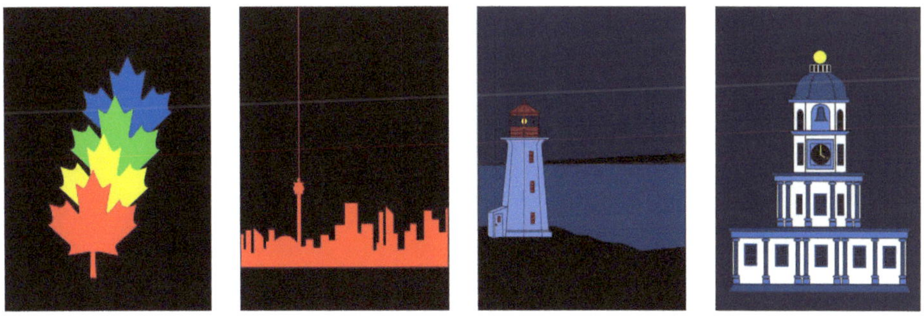

New York – Buffalo

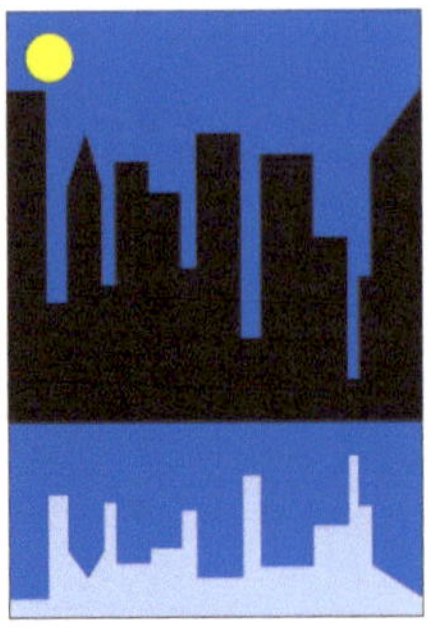

Chicago

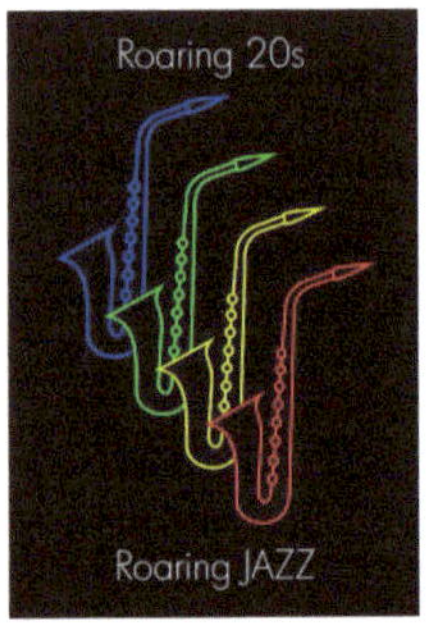

Denver - Portland - San Francisco

Portland

San Francisco

Grand Canyon

Nashville – Inspired by Lyrics

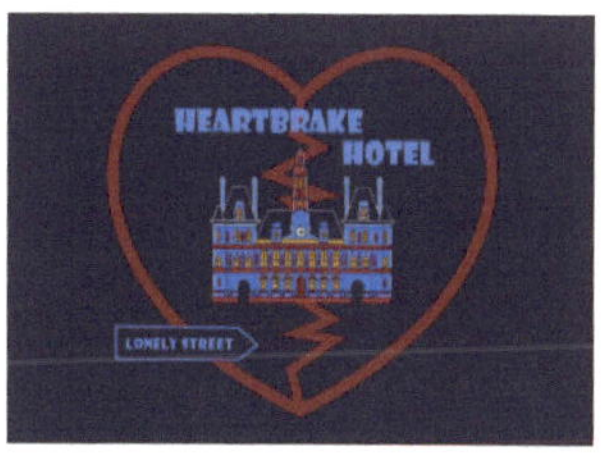

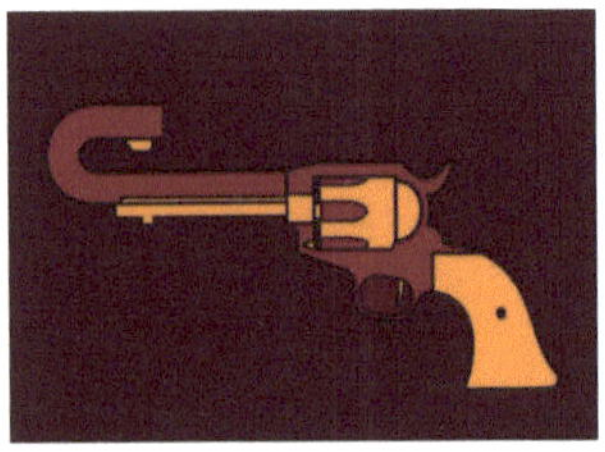

The South America Collection

Caminito Boca Buenos Aires Argentina

aster Island Chile

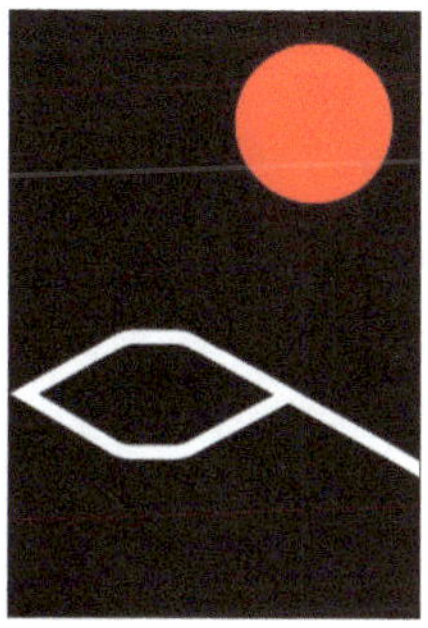

The East and far East Collection

Japan - Golden Pavilion - Tokyo Tower - Ginza - Fuji - Tokyo Portal
Japan

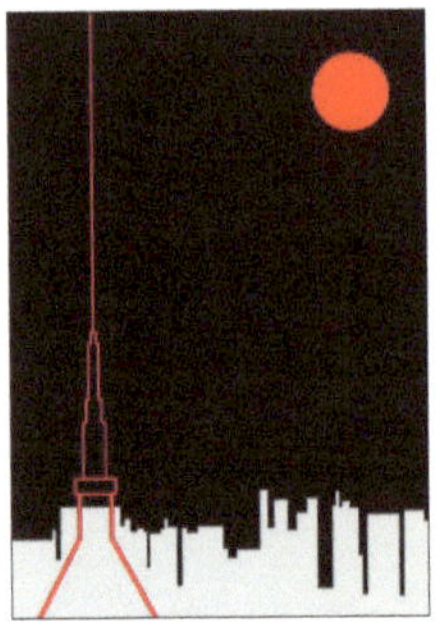

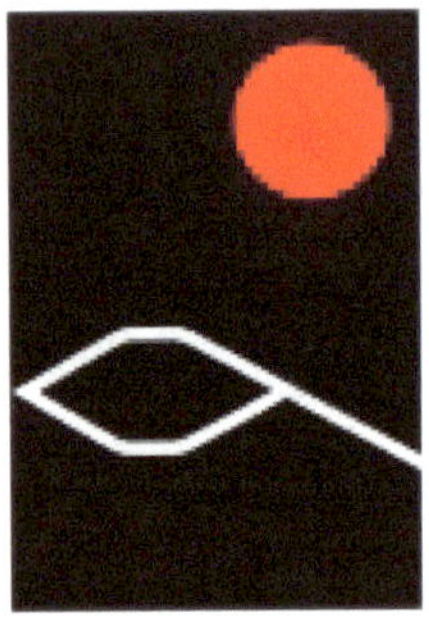

China
Confucius - Shanghai - Pudong - Wild Goose Pagoda - Temple of Longhua - Great Wall of China

China - My Calligraphy - Chinese letters for “Fish”, for “Dog”, and for “Us”

Hans Christian Andersen

India - Taj Mahal

Mount Everest Nepal

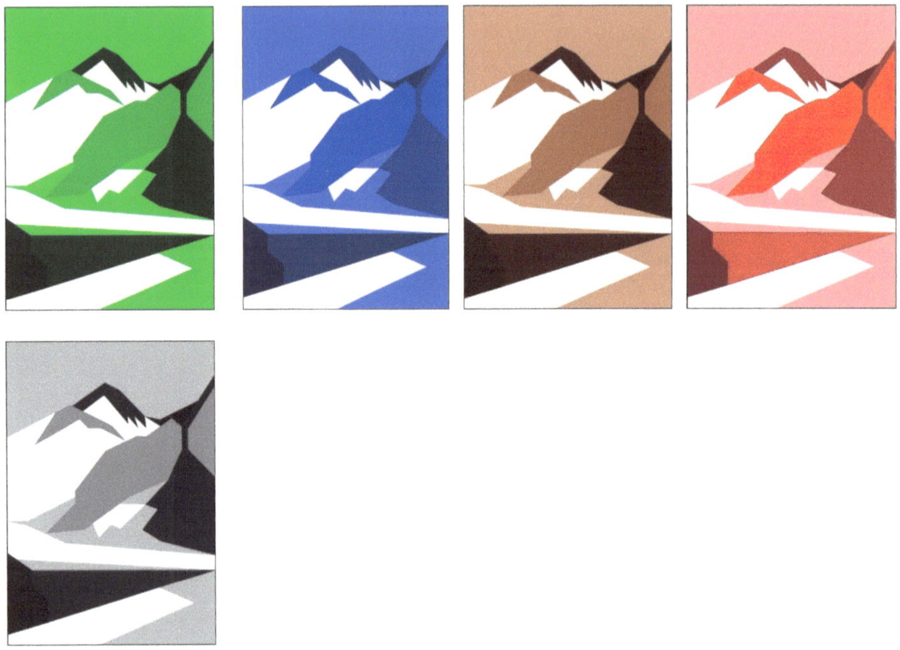

The Australia/Oceania and Collection

Sydney Opera House and Sydney Harbor Bridge - Sydney Opera House - Pig Face Butterfly Fish - Kangaroo

The Africa Collection

South Africa

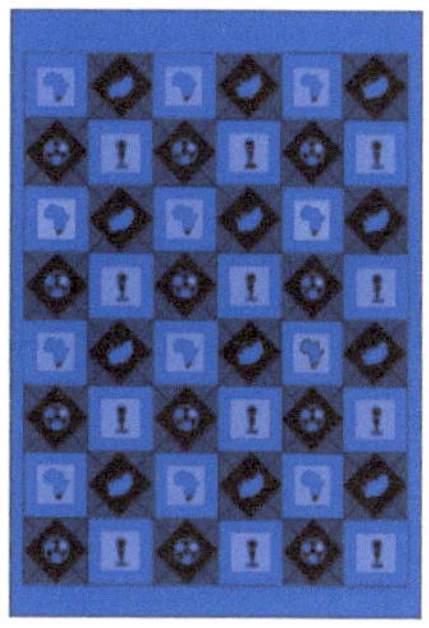

For sale after 31 October 2010 - After clearing with MMX Art, Cape Town

The Miscellaneous Collection

Architecture

Circus

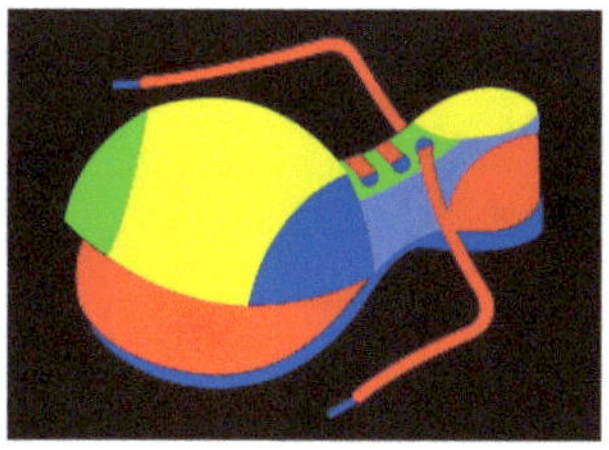

Museums - Cathedrals - Churches – Christianity

Churches – Christianity

Hans Christian Andersen illustrations

Sculptural and Aesthetic Vintage Cars - Racing Cars - Motor Cycles

Vintage Cars

Racing Cars

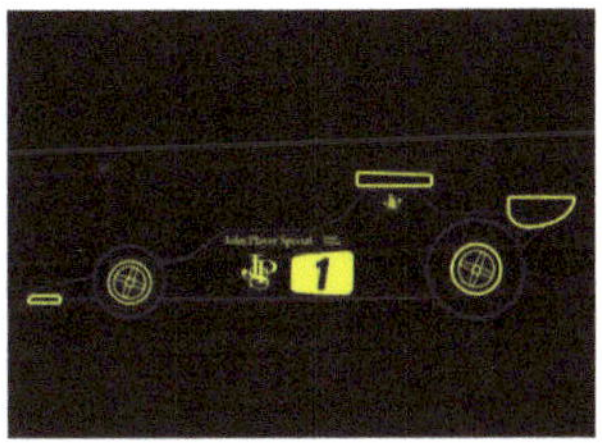

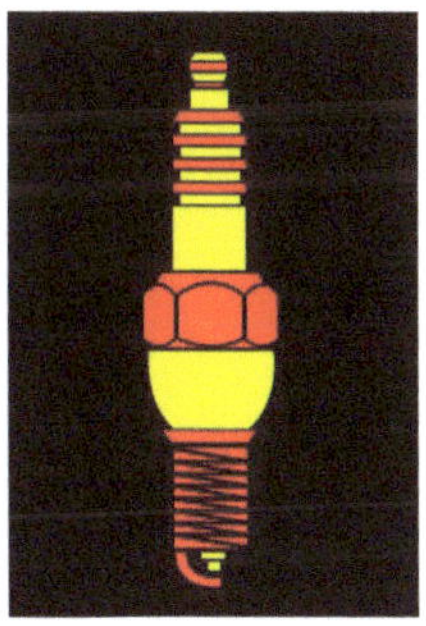

Motor Cycles

Wind Power

Flowers

Fairy Tale Characters from my Fairy Tales

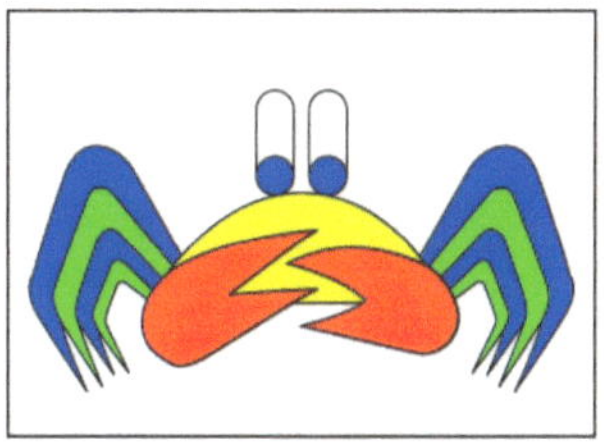

Special Selection - Visual Knowledge - Lonvig by Minymo – Dantrout

The Owner's Collection

Not for general sale.
For sale to the Owners.

Palaces, Manor Houses etc.

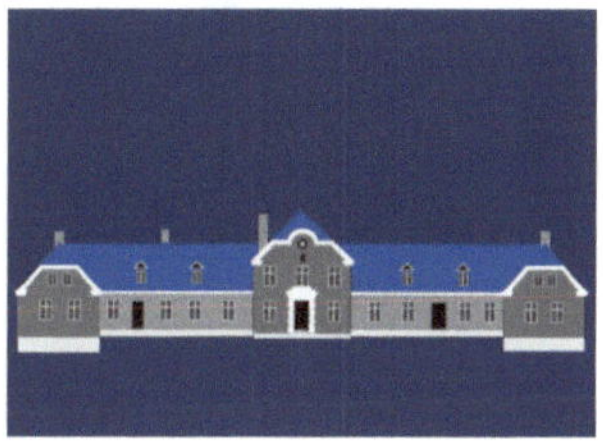

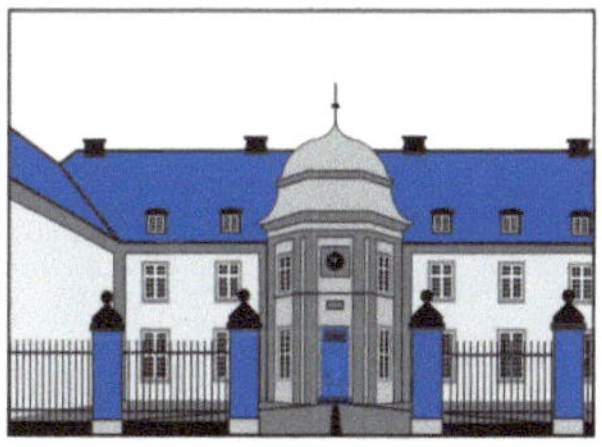

Palaces, Manor Houses etc (continued)

Legends

To be cleared with the family of sculptor Edvard Eriksen and New Coat of Arms for Paris cleared with Mayor Bertrand Delanoë.

Adding new motifs to the 325+ artworks
Artworks will continually be added to the collections of 325+ artworks. Ideas from you are welcome on lonvig@mail.dk

Commissioned art work
My work for companies, public and private bodies, financial institutions, ministries etc. is continued parallel with adding to the 325+ motifs. I often work on an entrepreneur basis. As an entrepreneur I create individual motifs to customers for different applications. .
For instance stamps to US Postal, posters etc. for the Children's Museum in Las Vegas, fine art motifs to TOPTEN exhibition in Rome, and design jobs for Bang & Olufsen.

Collecting

Digital art has become trendy.
And.
I can use IT in the entire art process - including fine art print with high quality and high sustainability - even in my own art studio...the latest adjustments to my studio configuration has closed a ring of developments that began 10 years ago.
YES, sure I'm a lucky devil...Nothing Less. I am even a lucky bastard.
My friend Carsten Thomsen is a lucky bastard, too. Carsten Thomsen and I have worked with the synergy effects of music and visual art in art events. Carsten Thomsen has a master degree from The Royal Danish Academy of Music.
I can best compare my feelings after having installed the Technical Prerequisites with the feelings of a pianist achieving to buy his first Steinway & Sons Grand Piano and install it in his music room. Some years ago, Carsten Thomsen bought his first Steinway & Sons Piano. He was just happy. He even felt he had never played that well. Likewise, I feel that I have never created fine art that well. My pianist friend said that he could not in decency play badly on his Steinway & Sons. Likewise, I feel that I cannot in decency create anything less than the best using "My new Steinway & Sons". Steinway & Sons is probably one of the greatest brands on Earth.

A Steinway & Sons Grand Piano is the finest that you can get. My new "Steinway & Sons" gives me the opportunity to make the best artworks possible*.

Asbjorn Lonvig, artist
Lille Fejringhus
43 Fejringhusvej
8722 Hedensted
Denmark

The Temple of The Golden Pavilion
Kyoto Japan

Kinkaku-ji (金閣寺 Temple of the Golden Pavilion?), also known as Rokuon-ji (鹿苑寺 Deer Garden Temple?), is a Zen Buddhist temple in Kyoto, Japan. The garden complex is an excellent example of Muromachi period garden design. It is designated as a National Special Historic Site and a National Special Landscape, and it is one of 17 locations comprising the Historic Monuments of Ancient Kyoto World Heritage Site. It is also one of the most popular buildings in Japan, attracting a large number of visitors annually.

Next Step

The natural continuation of this book
is my website lonvig.dk
On this website you will find thumbnails
of all 325+ motifs - click on a thumbnail
and see enlargements, descriptions, and videos.

Quick Response code (QR code)
lonvig.dk

My Next Book:
Art Beyond Bounds.

I think "Art Beyond Bounds" by many traditional art lovers will be categorized as controversial.
I am sure the traditional art lovers will not sing my praises.
I am sure the traditional art lovers probably prefer art is executed by a painter using brush, a palette with oil paint, and a canvas on an aisle.
He/she might even wear a Basque beret and a white smock with paint stains.

The digital painter does not use a brush, a palette, oil paint, and a canvas on an aisle.
I have performed a series of tests.
You prepare a Digital Painting in an Image Management System (Photoshop, Paint Shop Pro etc.)
Then you define a set of parameters and an IT-system does the hard work.
On the screen you can follow the digital painting coming to existence.
It is amazing to look at - you can see the strokes being done with breakneck speed.
It only lasts for a few seconds or minutes.
You can see the result in seconds/minutes and if it is not satisfactory you alter some parameters and the IT-system computer tries.

Art is not about tools.
You pick the tools you want, what matters is the quality of the final product.
By using IT-Technology you make the same or better results.
How to define parameters is the essential.
How to manage the software
This is not at all an easy task.
You have to learn and practice parameter definition over and over again.
It takes a huge effort to master parameter definition to perfection.
On the other hand, if you master parameter definition to perfection you might be able to create Art Beyond Bounds.
My intention is to improve my skills and become a master in parameter definition to perfection.
If I succeed I might then one day create Art Beyond Bounds.

All of the above is told about in the book: "Art Beyond Bounds".
In order not to confuse my Colorful Simplicity style - which has become my brand - with all the different styles in Digital Painting, the Digital Painting is done by *Ozborne-Whilliamsson, Ozborne-W., or Ozborne - my alias in this matter.*
Osborne is the English for Asbjorn.
William is the English for Vilhelm, which was my father's name.
Then Whilliamsson is the son of Vilhelm.
The z in Ozborne is a tribute to a certain Ozzy, you know the "Godfather of Heavy Metal", Ozzy Osborne.
Ozzie's surname is the same as my alias Christian name.
Ozzy is an artist, so am I.
Ozzy opposes standards of behavior, so do I.
There is a connection.
The psychologist C.G.Jung would argue that this is not coincidental.
It is due to a "Collective Unconscious" that steers many aspects of our lives.
Now.
When you search on "Ozborne Whilliamsson" you will only have hits belonging to me.

Ponte Veccio
by Ozborne-Whillimsson

Cinque Terre
by Ozborne-W.

Polar Night
by Ozborne

www.ingramcontent.com/pod-product-compliance
Lightning Source LLC
Chambersburg PA
CBHW041322210926
51847CB00002B/19